One Mile At A Time

You're not just a number on a screen. You're a life that Matters

Dedication

For the men and women in the trucking industry who feel unseen, unheard, and forgotten.

I care about you.
I feel you.
I hear you.
*But most of all—I **see** you.*
And you matter.

—Jason

Author's Note

This book wasn't written to be pretty. It was written to be honest.

Everything here—the raw moments, the breakdowns, the small victories—is from my life.

I didn't write this because I had it all figured out. I wrote this because I didn't.

If you're in the middle of your own storm, I hope these words help you feel less alone.

And if you've made it out the other side, I hope you'll remember how it felt.

We all carry something. This is what I carried.

—Jason

Chapter 1 Hi, I'm Jason

Hi, I'm Jason. Nice to meet you.

I'm a long-haul trucker, a drone pilot, a storyteller—and just a guy trying to make sense of the wreckage. I've spent more nights sleeping in the back of a semi than I can count, chasing paychecks and sunsets, chasing time I couldn't get back. I've been through divorce before, but this one? This one broke something in me I didn't know could break.

I'm not here to write a redemption story or some perfect guide to healing. I'm here to tell the truth. I want you to know this isn't written from a distance, after the dust has settled. This was written with bruised hands and tired eyes, from truck stop parking lots and cold bunks. I started this journal when I had nothing left but questions, heartbreak, and the ghost of someone I used to call my best friend. And I kept going—one mile at a time.

There were nights I sat in my truck, staring out at the rain, thinking the world might be better off without me. I'd scroll through Facebook looking for comfort and instead find posts that made me hate myself more—confirmation bias disguised as truth. Words that echoed every lie my own mind was already screaming: *You failed. You ruined it. You deserve this.* And in those moments, I didn't know how to reach out. Not because I didn't want help— but because I didn't even know what help would look like. How do you ask someone to carry what you can't name?

If you've been there—if you've questioned your worth, if you've believed you were the villain in your own story—then this book is for you. Because I've sat in that same darkness, whispering the same prayers, hoping for just one reason to try again in the morning.

And sometimes... one reason showed up. A stranger's voice on a short video saying, "You matter." A friend who texted just when the silence felt too loud. Or maybe it was just the idea of taking *one more step*, even if I didn't know where it would lead.

This story isn't finished. I'm still walking it, still stumbling, still learning how to forgive myself and find some peace in the pieces. But I believe there's someone out there who needs to hear this. Someone sitting alone in a truck stop, or a bedroom, or on a break at work—trying to hold it together. And if that's you, I want you to know: I see you. I *am* you.

We'll walk this one step, one mile, at a time.

Together.

Chapter 2 No One Asks If You're Okay (Just If the Load Made It on Time)

There's a unique kind of silence that comes from sitting behind the wheel of a semi with a shattered heart and a job that doesn't care. You could be halfway through a breakdown, halfway across the country, and the only thing anyone wants to know is whether you're on schedule.

Even if your company genuinely cares, the *industry* doesn't. There's no formal support system for truck drivers going through personal crisis. No mental health resource button built into the ELD. No standard protocol for how to ask if a driver is okay—just protocols for whether the freight is moving.

According to a 2023 report from the CDC, truck drivers have one of the highest suicide rates among any profession in the U.S. And yet, when we talk about safety in this job, it's always about brakes, hours of service, and inspections. We don't talk about the man in the cab who hasn't eaten in 18 hours because his brain's too fogged over with grief. Or the woman staring at her wedding ring between shifter pulls because her home life just crumbled. We don't talk about how silence in a sleeper berth can become unbearable when your whole life is falling apart.

There was a stretch—days into my own unraveling—when I realized I had gone nearly an entire day without eating. I'd been drinking water, but food? I couldn't even process the idea of it. There wasn't an appetite to forget—just an absence of function. All I could do was drive, cry, and try not to collapse under the weight of everything I was carrying.

The music made it worse. I was playing songs that matched every dark thought I had about myself. Songs that validated the self-hate. Songs that told me I *deserved* to be alone. And mile after mile, I believed them. The tears were just part of the routine. Freight had to get delivered. That's what mattered. Not the man behind the wheel.

And what happens if you miss that delivery window? Maybe someone doesn't get their shipment. Maybe there's a fee. Maybe dispatch gets frustrated. Maybe you lose that lane. But *no one* ever says, "Are you okay?" Not really. Not if they're being honest.

There was a night—not long ago—where I sat in my truck after a long conversation where I laid out everything. The good, the bad, the broken. I told someone I trusted that I didn't think I deserved grace. That I *was* the villain in my own story. That everything that happened to me was a consequence I'd earned.

And they didn't accept that. They didn't give me some speech full of sunshine or empty reassurance. They just stayed with me. They reminded me I was still showing up. Still fighting. Still driving. Still here. And maybe that's the point. That when everything else is stripped away, what matters isn't being perfect. It's just being *present*—even when it hurts.

The industry will never tell you this, but I will: your feelings matter. You are more than your deliveries. And there's no shame in saying you're not okay.

This chapter isn't here to solve everything. It's here so someone like you knows that what you're feeling isn't weak or rare or selfish.

It's *human*.

And you're still allowed to take this one mile at a time.

Chapter 3 Rituals and Ruins—Counting the Tomorrows

"There was a last time for everything — but I didn't know it then. The last time you called, the last time we laughed, the last time that I held your hand without knowing I would never hold it again. Funny, how the end never tells you that it's arrived — it just stands there quietly at the door, waiting for you to notice."
— K. Ashley
(This quote has been the wallpaper on my phone since March.)

Rituals are how we count time when the clock doesn't help. For Haley and me, they weren't just traditions—they were anchors. Lifelines. Little promises we kept no matter what the world threw at us. And as I sit with the wreckage of what's no longer ours, it's those rituals that haunt me most. They're where love lived.

When I was on the road, we'd wake up together almost every morning through video chat—her at home, me in the truck. She'd have her coffee, I'd have mine, and we'd greet the day like it belonged to both of us. At night, I'd toss my phone onto the bed in the sleeper cab like I was "throwing her," something she'd laugh at every time. Then came the attack kisses—our thing. I rarely missed a morning, and if I was driving late into the night, I'd pull over just so she wouldn't miss them either. Even thousands of miles apart, we built a rhythm—one step, one sip, one kiss at a time.

Camping was more than a vacation—it was the heart of our year. We planned everything around it. When we finally upgraded to a fifth-wheel RV, it felt like winning at life. I didn't care about luxury or showing off—it was the dream Haley and I built from the ground up.

We fished the Menominee River like it was our second home. That river carried our laughter and our quiet moments, side by side in folding chairs, lines in the water, hearts full.

Our first trip together, back when we were dating, was with my old Nomad travel trailer. It was rough around the edges, but it was mine—and that meant everything to me. Haley didn't see a leaky roof; she saw a future. We made it one night before the air conditioning started leaking water all over the bed. Her frustration showed, but she didn't yell or blame—she just looked at me, and together, we decided to trade it in. We left that lot with a brand-new Springdale. She was glowing—smiling so wide I don't think I even saw her that happy on our wedding day. I stayed quiet at the dealership because her joy said everything. That's what mattered: she was happy.

Her birthday, our anniversary—those were sacred. I'd miss every major holiday before I'd miss those days. Two years ago, we spent her birthday at the Kalahari in Wisconsin Dells. Somewhere along the way she found a roadside stand to pan for gems, and when she discovered a purple stone, she lit up like a kid. We had it set into a ring she wore constantly. It wasn't about jewelry—it was about a moment, captured and worn close.

And then there were the truck door races. Every time we went somewhere in the pickup, I'd rush to beat her to the door. She'd play along, pretending to go for it, and I'd nudge her aside with a grin and say, "You should never have to open the door." At night, if we passed glass buildings or gas station windows, we'd glance at our reflection and say, "Sexy truck." No one else got that. It was ours. It still is—just now it echoes.

The rituals never warned me when they were happening for the last time. No flashing lights. No alarms. Just quiet endings disguised as regular days. And now, I count the tomorrows not by the calendar, but by the ache of their absence.

Chapter 4 Home Isn't Home, and the Work Visits Are Gone

There's a quiet ache in coming home to a place that used to carry laughter, clutter, and all the noise of a life shared—but now just echoes your own footsteps.

I used to get excited driving home. I'd get ready to leave the yard to come home, message her that I was on my way, and she'd reply, *"Yayyy! I gets all the kisses!"*
I'd say *"Maybe."*
She'd send back *"Huffs."*
That was our little dance. Our rhythm.

She'd meet me outside, help unload, sometimes have dinner waiting, and no matter how the house looked—clean or messy, dog hair or dishes—it didn't matter. I had *her*. She'd give me those back scritch hugs that melted the stress right off my spine. The kind of embrace that said: *"You're safe now."*

Even in the little things, she made it feel like home. There was a gravel area in front of the house that flooded with snowmelt or rain. She called it "the moat." She'd usually park in a way that made it easier for me to get inside—sometimes forgetting, but always apologizing when she did. She was thoughtful like that.

And we had our rituals. Silly to some, sacred to us.

Every time we got into the truck together, I'd rush to the passenger side to open the door before she could. She'd pretend to grab the handle, and I'd gently push her aside with a smirk:
"You should never have to open your own door."

At night, when we'd drive past a glass building or store window, we'd glance at our reflection and grin.

"*Sexy truck,*" we'd say in unison, and laugh like we were kids.

We were so *us* in those moments.

Before we got married, when she still lived in the Madison area and I was living up north, she'd drive an hour up to the yard in Westfield just to see me after work. I'd be sitting there, parked overnight, prepping to run locals the next morning. But she made the trip just to spend time with me—because *that* was her love language. Showing up. Being present.

Sometimes, she'd even drive all the way to my house at two in the morning—three and a half hours each way—just to spend a single day together before heading back to Madison. That kind of effort is rare. But for her, it wasn't about grand gestures—it was about *us*. She made the yard a refuge. She made home feel alive. And she showed me, over and over, what commitment looked like when it was *real*.

And I'll never forget the time I was parked at a Kwik Trip near Milwaukee, absolutely miserable. I had a fever, a terrible cough—I was wrecked. I told her not to come, warned her she'd get sick too. But she did what she always did—she came anyway.

She stepped into my truck like it was her mission to heal me. She wiped down every surface, cleaned everything top to bottom, trying to clear the germs out of the space. Then she laid with me. Rubbed her hand across my forehead. Stayed by my side. No fear. No complaints. Just presence.
She made me feel seen, whole. Like a human being—not just a driver behind a wheel.

I can still see the outline of her hand on the window as she left.

I didn't know then that those days would become relics. That one day, I'd walk into this house and it wouldn't smell like her shampoo or her cooking, but like nothing. Like air. Like absence.

Now, I come home to silence. No messages. No "huffs." No arms waiting to wrap around me. I walk through the same doors and drop my bags by the wall, and the house doesn't greet me.

The rituals are gone.

The gravel is just gravel.
The door is just a door.
The reflection in the window is just me.

And the worst part?

I don't even know when the last time was. The last time we laughed. The last time we shared coffee. The last time she reached for my hand and I didn't know it would be the *final* time.

Love doesn't end with a gunshot or a scream. It ends with a whisper. With a missed coffee. A text that never comes. A door that never opens again.

The world outside keeps turning like nothing happened. But inside, every room remembers. Every silence screams.

And no matter how many miles I drive, I can't seem to outrun that truth.

Chapter 5 Friends and Family Try to Help, But They Don't Understand How Much Pain Is Truly Inside

When the sky begins to darken inside your chest, and you're just trying to survive one hour at a time, people show up. They text. They call. They offer to listen. They want to help. And you want to let them—God, you want to let them—but you don't even know what to ask for. How do you explain a pain that you can't put into words? How do you tell them that nothing will fix it, but it still means everything that they're trying?

In the early days, after the split, my phone didn't stay silent. Steve Brown, a guy I used to work with at Brakebush, called me out of the blue. I hadn't heard from him in forever, but he saw the post I made on Facebook about the divorce, and he called just to talk. Logical and matter-of-fact, kind of like my dad. We talked for about an hour. It wasn't emotional, but it was steady—and sometimes, that kind of steadiness is what keeps you grounded when you feel like you're drifting.

Jason Gustafson, my best friend from high school and someone who lived just down the street when I moved into this house, texted me. Simple check-in. No pressure. Just a "you okay?" that meant more than he probably realized.

Then there was Ryan Vlk.

Ryan was different.

He called every day. He didn't stop calling, even when I had nothing to say. Even when I yelled, or cried, or vented things I didn't even understand myself. He had been my trainee once, but over time he became more like a brother. I wasn't always fair to him, but I think he understood. I think he knew I was just trying to breathe, and sometimes the only way to do that was to lose my cool in a place that felt safe. And Ryan gave me that place.

The support didn't stop there. My bosses—Chris Stenske, Mark Borud, Norlene Grey, Chris Armstrong—they all offered me their numbers. Every one of them. Especially Chris Stenske. He told me, "Call me anytime. If you need to yell, scream, whatever, just call me." Not every workplace does that. Not every supervisor opens that kind of door. But they did.

Even my dad and stepmom called regularly. My dad isn't the emotional type. He's logical. Steady. Practical. And while sometimes that rubbed up against the emotional chaos I was living in, I knew it came from love. Some days I couldn't talk. I'd just tell them it was a bad day. They respected that.

But here's the hard truth: no matter how many people offer you help, this kind of pain lives alone.

And it isn't because others don't care—it's because even when they do, they still can't crawl into the exact shape of your grief. They don't know what it feels like to have your identity stripped away, to be 47 and staring down a life that no longer exists. People would say, "You'll feel better after the hearing," like there's a switch that flips. Like in eight tomorrows, the ache will lift.

But they don't see what I see. They don't feel what I feel. That day in court—it isn't just a date on a calendar. It's the funeral of the future I built in my mind. And when the gavel drops, my old life dies. My identity as "Haley's husband" dies. And the only thing left is... what now?

People mean well. I've never doubted that. But this chapter isn't about answers—it's about truth. And the truth is, when you're drowning, even the brightest flashlight can feel like it's being held a mile away. You still have to swim to it.

And I'm still swimming.

Chapter 6 My Demons Don't Knock—They Kick Down the Door

This chapter isn't about pity. It's about truth.

Because I know I'm not alone.

There are drivers out there right now, parked behind a Love's truck stop, staring at their steering wheels, wondering if anyone would care if they didn't wake up. I see you. I was you. And if you're reading this, I need you to hear this next part like it's being screamed through your radio speakers:

You are not alone. You are not too far gone. And you don't have to fix everything tonight.

There were nights I would drive in silence, or worse—I'd put on music that fed the self-hate. Songs that made me feel like the pain was justified. Like it belonged to me. That I deserved to feel this way. I would clench the wheel so tight my knuckles would go white, and tears would be streaming down my face on I-90 while I delivered freight to a world that didn't even know I was falling apart.

Because here's the truth: as long as the freight gets delivered, no one asks if you're okay.

Even if your company cares—and I'm lucky that mine does—the industry doesn't. You're not seen as human. You're a set of drive time hours. A number on a dispatch screen. You could be collapsing emotionally or mentally, but as long as the load shows up on time, you've "done your job."

I remember one day I'd been driving all night. I forgot to eat. Not because I was pushing for time or trying to shave off minutes on the clock, but because I simply couldn't function. I'd drink water, but food? It didn't even register. I'd park, and I wouldn't sleep—I'd just sit there, numb. Mind spiraling. Wondering if this was it. If this was what the rest of my life was going to feel like.

I dropped nearly forty pounds in just a few months. Not from diet or exercise. From grief. From stress. From heartbreak. I started the year at 221. I'm down to 183 now. And the worst part is that some people will look at that and say, "Good for you." But it wasn't a transformation. It was a symptom.

The worst nights were the ones I thought I deserved it.

That I was the villain in the story.

You've read the story so far. You've seen the memories, the pain, the heartbreak—but I promise you, there was a night just a few weeks ago where I told the very AI writing this book with me that I was the true villain. That all of it was my fault. And I argued that point like my life depended on proving it.

Because in my mind, it did.

When you're that deep in the spiral, logic doesn't matter. The good you've done vanishes. All you can see is the damage. You think of every time you could have been better. You question whether anyone ever really loved you—or if maybe you were always too broken to be loved the way you needed. You put yourself on trial in your own mind, and the verdict is always: guilty.

The guilt grows roots.

What saved me? Sometimes it wasn't friends or family or even God. Sometimes it was four strangers on the internet. Just people with phones and cameras who knew how to speak life to someone falling apart.

They weren't therapists. They weren't trained. But they posted videos for people like me. Just a minute or two, telling us to hold on. Reminding us the world might still have something kind in it. One of them would even act like he brought you coffee, and for a second, it felt like Haley was handing it to me again.

That's how fragile I was. That something so small could keep me tethered.

I'll tell you about them later. They deserve their own chapter.

Because some nights I sat in that bunk praying for God to take me home. Asking Him to end it. And the only thing that got me through was someone I didn't even know saying, "Just one more day. You made it this far. You're not done yet."

And I believed them—just enough to stay.

Just enough to keep breathing.

Just enough to take **one more mile. One more step. One more breath.**

Chapter 7 Radical Acceptance

One mile at a time isn't just a lifeline anymore—it's a direction.

I didn't have some grand revelation. No sunrise epiphany. No soft music playing in the background like in a movie. I just woke up one day and realized: the pain was still there, but the resistance was making it worse.

The bargaining, the hoping, the replaying of memories like maybe if I just found the right one, I'd unlock the cheat code to go back and fix everything. None of it worked. None of it brought her back. None of it changed the silence in the house or the ache in my chest. The only thing it did was keep me stuck in a story that had already ended.

So I stopped.

Not because I wanted to, but because I couldn't carry the weight of it anymore. That's when I learned what *radical acceptance* really means. It's not agreeing with what happened. It's not being okay with it. It's not saying it was fair.

It's saying:

"This is the truth. Now what?"

I had to accept that the life I had is gone. That the woman I loved has moved on. That the house is quiet not because something's broken, but because this is the new reality.

And the truth hit hardest one day in the quietest way.

That morning, I watched a video from *Ethan Original*. He was working on a car, talking like he always does—just a guy sharing his thoughts while doing something ordinary. But then he said it:

"If nothing changes, nothing changes."

That line hit like a freight train. It followed me through the entire day. I couldn't stop hearing it—like a mantra I'd never been told before, but somehow had always needed. I didn't know why it shook me the way it did. I just knew it wouldn't let go.

That night, I sat quietly and talked to the AI helping me write this book. I wasn't angry. I wasn't hopeful. I wasn't sad.
I was just *present*.

That might've been the first time in months that I wasn't spiraling through guilt or trying to negotiate with the past. I wasn't looking for someone to blame—not her, not myself. I was just sitting in what *was*. And when I said those words aloud—*if nothing changes, nothing changes*—I realized that something *had* changed.

Me.

I wasn't begging for a different ending anymore. I wasn't resisting the truth. I was facing it.

That moment cracked something open in me. I stopped asking why.
I stopped trying to bargain with ghosts.
And instead, I started doing the scariest thing of all—
I *sat with it*.

The grief.
The guilt.
The quiet routines I now do alone.

And slowly—quietly—I started noticing something else:
I was still breathing.

I didn't know what came next. I still don't. But I knew I wasn't going to keep trying to live in a past that no longer existed. There's no roadmap for this part. There's no right way to start over. But this chapter—this *mile*—is where I began to let go of what I thought should be, and started accepting what *is*.

I'm still learning how to be okay with not being okay.

Still learning how to show up for a life that doesn't look anything like the one I planned.

Still reminding myself: just because something hurts, doesn't mean you failed.

Acceptance isn't the end of grief. It's the beginning of peace.

And for me, peace didn't look like joy or relief.

It looked like stopping the fight.

It looked like sitting in the driver's seat, hands loose on the wheel, finally telling myself:

"This happened. It hurt. But I'm still here."

Chapter 8 D-Day

I know what the court says this is: a dissolution of marriage.
I know what the state calls it: a legal process.
But to me? It's the slow, scheduled funeral of everything I once called home.

June 12th. That's the date circled on the calendar. The day the gavel falls. The day the story changes from "we" to "was." And if you've never had to count down the days to your own goodbye, let me tell you—it doesn't feel like closure. It feels like staring at a bomb with a digital timer and no way to defuse it.

June 12, 2025

There are no sirens, no dramatic music, no cinematic lead-up. Just 4:07 AM and the sound of my own breath as I stared at the ceiling of the RV, already wide awake and unable to move. The day had finally come. D-Day. Divorce Day. And despite all the miles, all the reflection, all the preparation... nothing could prepare me for what this day would feel like.

I stepped outside into the quiet campground, coffee in hand, as the birds broke the silence before the sun did. It was a ritual I used to share with myself—sitting in my old garage, watching the light rise slowly—but this morning it was different. This morning I was writing a eulogy.

Not for Haley. Not for me. For the marriage.

Five years ago to the day, we were side by side on a pontoon boat, floating the Menominee River between Wisconsin and Michigan, pulling in bluegill after bluegill and laughing like the world couldn't touch us. It was one of those perfect days that etches itself into your soul whether you ask it to or not. Even in the midst of COVID, when the world said don't go out, don't gather, don't live—we lived. Because that's what love does when it's real. It finds the quiet in chaos and builds something sacred in it.

That was June 12, 2020.

This is June 12, 2025.

This is the day we mourn what was sacred, and say goodbye to what we can never quite explain to others. This is the day I wrote a eulogy to post on Facebook, honoring the death of something that never stopped meaning everything to me, yet I never posted it.

By the time 1:00 PM arrived, I was dressed in my best—slacks, shirt, tie. I looked like I was going to a funeral. And in a way, I was. But there was no casket, no funeral director, only a cold courtroom with no one there to mourn other than myself.

My lawyer and I were seated at the table on the right—but there was nothing right about what was happening. The courtroom was real. The pain was real. And Haley—the woman I had promised my forever to—was on Zoom, visible on a screen across the room, calm and unreadable. I recognized her surroundings—her car, parked outside her parents' house. The same place where we used to video chat every day when we were dating. Full circle. Painfully so.

When it was my turn to speak, I answered the questions like I was supposed to. Mechanically. Because what else could I do? No one in that room asked how my heart was doing. No one cared what five years of memories had done to my chest, my voice, my sense of home. All they wanted were signatures. Boxes checked. Confirmation that the marriage was, in their words, "irretrievably broken."

But it wasn't broken. It was buried. And I was the one left holding the shovel.

As the hearing ended, Haley's screen went black. No goodbye. No final words. Just silence. That was it.

I walked with my lawyer to the clerk's office. He handed me the divorce decree, shook my hand, and said, "It's done. Say hi to your dad for me."

Done.

Like we were something to be filed away.

I returned to the RV and immediately peeled off the formal clothes. They didn't belong on me anymore. I put on the oversized Carhartt hoodie that still smelled like her. The one she used to steal from my closet and curl into when we camped together.

Then I sat.

And I cried.

There was no relief. No fresh start. No weight lifted. Just an overwhelming sense of finality. I didn't want to drink. I didn't want to talk. I didn't want to move. I just wanted to go back to that boat, five years ago, and tell those two people to hold on tighter.

But we can't go back. We can only grieve forward.

That night, I found the old wedding signs in the trailer—the ones we used to hang outside the Springdale before we traded it in for the fifth wheel we called the "big baby." They were supposed to go in the fire. That was my plan. But instead, I set them aside to go in the basement. A quiet little corner of the shrine to the life we built together.

Because for all that went wrong, that part was real.

And as I sit with the silence in this RV, and the distance between us stretches beyond 230 miles, I know this:
No matter what the judge says, I will never be able to explain how it feels to sign your name under a line that declares you're no longer someone's husband.

The night ended in tears, music, and a moment of silence I didn't break. I listened to the songs I wrote months earlier, never realizing how perfectly they would score the worst day of my life. One of them, "Goodbye My Forever," played on repeat:

Goodbye my forever love
Like a fallen angel from above
You were my everything, my sky
Now it's time to say goodbye

It hurt. All of it. Every line. Every word. Every second of that day.

But I survived it.

Reflection

D-Day wasn't about destruction. It was about surrender. Letting go of the version of love I clung to with bleeding hands.

It was the day I became a divorced man. But more than that, it was the day I admitted to myself that I still loved her. Still do. Always will.

And maybe, just maybe, that love—even in its brokenness—can help someone else survive their own D-Day.

Because the truth is, I didn't write this chapter for closure. I wrote it so that someone else, sitting in their truck or lying on their floor or staring at a screen with a marriage dissolving on the other side, will know this:

You're not crazy for feeling like the world ended.
You're not weak for wishing it hadn't.
And you are not alone.

The paperwork doesn't care about memories.
The hearing won't ask about camping trips, or Sunday mornings, or promises made in the middle of the night between two people.
There's no checkbox for the pain in your chest when you realize that no matter how hard you loved, some things still fall apart.

There's no manual for how to grieve someone who's still alive.
There's no protocol for how to untangle your soul from another person's without bleeding.

D-Day doesn't mean you failed.
It just means the chapter ended before the story did.

But I will show up.
Because this chapter isn't just about the legal ending of a marriage.
It's about the beginning of whatever comes after.
And I don't know what that is yet. But I'll find out—

One breath,
One step,
One mile at a time.

Chapter 9 Radical Truths

At some point in healing, you stop flailing in the wreckage and start looking in the mirror—not to punish yourself, but to finally understand the part you played. The truths you avoided. The pain you caused. The signs you missed. The apologies you never said out loud.

This is that point for me.

But here's the thing—I never really saw myself as the victim. Not deep down. I always had this gnawing voice in my head that said, *You're the villain in this story*. And maybe I didn't argue with it enough. Maybe because there were parts of it that felt too true.

I criticized her for the house being messy, especially once we got the dog. I let resentment build when the dishes piled up or the dog hair collected, and instead of talking about it from a place of love, I'd let the frustration slip through my tone.

I told her she never left her office. I made her feel lazy.

Her weight became something I didn't talk to her about with grace—I let it bother me, and then I withheld intimacy. I shut down when what she needed was closeness, and I justified it in my head like it was her fault.

She would ask to cuddle on the couch, and I'd brush her off—*"I have too much to do."*

And what was I doing?

Editing a video for a drone YouTube channel. *JJDrones*. Something that, looking back, should have been secondary to love. But I made it a priority. I used it as an excuse. *"I have to get this done or I'll miss my premiere."* As if some number on a screen mattered more than connection with the person sitting right there asking for my time.

When I bought the pickup truck to tow the fifth wheel, I didn't really talk it through with her. When I bought a drone, I didn't either. But when she spent money gambling, I was the first to call it irresponsible. To remind her it was a drain on our budget.

That's not partnership. That's hypocrisy.

And that's the radical truth:

There will be no monument to Saint Jason.

This is not a redemption arc. This is the unvarnished record of what I did, how it made her feel, and what I would give to do some of it differently.

I didn't always show up the way she needed. I didn't always prioritize her the way she deserved. I didn't always see what she was asking for behind the words.

And I miss her more for knowing that.

But this isn't about staying stuck in shame. Shame doesn't lead to healing. This is about clarity. About facing the truth so I never repeat these mistakes again—whether in a future relationship or just in how I treat the people I love from now on.

Radical truth is painful. But it's also freeing.

Because when you can tell your story without skipping the parts that make you squirm, you stop living in the shadows of what you hope people think you are—and start walking in the light of who you're finally becoming.

Reflection

I used to think the goal was to be forgiven. To make her see I was sorry. But maybe the real work is learning to forgive myself—not to let myself off the hook, but so I can carry this truth forward without letting it destroy me.

If nothing else, I want the man I become after this to be someone who never hides from hard truths again. Who listens. Who stays soft. Who doesn't confuse busy with present, or pride with protection.

I wasn't always the man I should have been. But I am trying to become him now.

And that matters, too.

Chapter 10 Four Men and a Cup of Coffee

I don't remember how I found them.

One night, sometime in the early spiral, I was parked alone. Tears wouldn't stop. Sleep wouldn't come. I was scrolling, mindlessly—Facebook, YouTube, Instagram, TikTok—trying to find anything that felt like hope.

And then there was a video.

Some guy standing outside a coffee shop saying, *"Hey, I brought you a cup."* He said he knew I'd probably had a hard day, that I didn't feel seen. He read a Bible verse. Prayed. It was barely a minute long.

I cried like someone had reached through the screen and touched my soul.

That man was **Josh Oldenburger**. A Canadian guy. He does this thing where he acts like he's sitting across from you, offering a warm cup of coffee and a few simple words that remind you—you still matter.

Then came **Kevin Lawson**. Calm voice. Deep eyes. His message wasn't flashy—it was grounding. Just quiet reminders to keep going, to let the waves pass, to hold on through the storm.

Youranxietyislying2you—a username that says it all. This man came across like the best friend you never knew you needed. No sugarcoating. Just truth, delivered with kindness. He made it okay to admit the shame. The fear. The nights I wasn't sure I wanted to keep doing this.

Then there was **Ethan Original**.

Ethan wasn't polished or performative. That's why I trusted him. One day he was working on a car and said, *"If nothing changes, nothing changes."* That line broke something open in me. I thought about it all day. I told ChatGPT about it that night. It wasn't just a phrase—it became a turning point. A mantra. The moment I started to truly accept what was happening, and stopped begging the past to come back.

Four men.

Strangers.

They didn't know I existed. They still don't. But they saved my life in pieces.

Because when you're a truck driver, parked behind a Love's at 2 a.m., with no one to talk to, no hugs waiting, no one asking how your heart is—you start to believe that you don't matter.

And then four men—across four different videos—say otherwise.

They say, *"You're not invisible. You're not broken beyond repair. You're not alone."*

And somehow, that's enough to make it one more mile.

Reflection: A Light Left On

When you're in that space—where your thoughts turn against you, where silence becomes a scream—it doesn't take a miracle to save you. It just takes someone being there. A voice. A face. A gesture as small as a stranger offering you coffee through a screen.

The world will never understand how much it matters when someone tells you, *"You made it. Now let's try again tomorrow."*

These four men didn't cure me. They didn't fix the gaping wound in my chest or make the memories stop showing up uninvited. But they offered me something no one else could in that moment: the permission to keep breathing. To stay. To hope there might still be a reason to.

Sometimes, what saves you doesn't know it's saving you.

This chapter isn't about content creators—it's about human beings. It's about those who decide to leave the light on for someone they'll never meet. And it's for the man sitting in his truck tonight, tears in his eyes, cigarette burning in his fingers, wondering if he matters.

You do.

I know it because I was you.

And if no one's told you yet—**I'll see you tomorrow.**

Chapter 11 Echo Chambers and Exit Signs — How Social Media Fuels the Spiral

There are a thousand things I wish I never saw.

And I don't mean pictures of her smiling, living a new life, or out with someone else. That's not what crushed me. What broke me were the things that told me she was *hurting*—and the sick, twisting feeling in my chest that whispered: *It's your fault.*

Meme after meme about worthlessness. Her profile picture was a cartoon rat holding a sign that said, "I'm worthless." Posts about being tired of life. About being exhausted from being strong for too long. And then, out of nowhere, she'd post something about going to a comedy club and having a great night—only to go back the next day to more memes that screamed quiet pain.

That's what hit hardest.

Because I know her. I know how she hides things in humor. I know how she speaks through screenshots and memes. And I would sit in the cab of my truck, staring at those posts, trying to breathe while the guilt sat like an anvil on my chest.

I did this.

I ruined her.

She was happy before me.

And now look at her.

That's what I believed. That's what social media told me. Not in words—but in patterns. In tone. In all the spaces between the lines.

And it didn't stop there.

Life360 nearly destroyed me.

I used to check it constantly. I would see where she was, how fast she was driving, what time she got home. Not because I was controlling—because I was desperate. I was grasping for any thread that might tell me she was okay. That she was surviving. But over time, it didn't bring me peace. It brought me torment.

I'd refresh it like a slot machine. Hoping she made it home safe. Hoping she didn't go somewhere that might suggest she was moving on. And every time I saw something I didn't understand, it would light a fuse under my heart.

Social media and Life360 didn't keep me connected—they kept me condemned.

It was like standing outside the house you once lived in, watching through the windows as everything burned, and believing the fire started in your own hands.

The Worst Kind of Spiral

I used to listen to a song called *"Better Off Without Me"* by Kyle Hume. And I didn't just listen to it—I weaponized it. I played it like I was trying to punish myself. Every word felt like a confession. Every chorus felt like a final verdict.

I didn't just think she'd be better off without me—I *believed* it.

I believed I was the reason she felt worthless.

That if I had just been better—more patient, more present, more kind—she wouldn't have sunk into this kind of pain. She wouldn't be making jokes about caffeine being her love language, or switching her profile picture to something that screamed self-loathing. She'd still be shining. Still be Haley.

I LOVE her.

Not *loved*. Not past tense.

I love her now.

And I probably always will.

And every time I saw her reduced to a meme or a cry for help, it broke me in ways I couldn't even explain. Because I knew I had contributed to the breaking.

Why I Had to Stop Looking

Eventually, I had to stop. Not because I didn't care—but because I *cared too much.*

Every glance pulled me deeper into the belief that *I ruined her life.* And when you're already living on a thread of survival, that belief is poison.

I had to stop watching her suffer in silence through a phone screen. I had to stop torturing myself with glimpses into a life that no longer included me—not because it didn't matter, but because I couldn't heal if I kept trying to carry her pain *and* mine.

That's the part no one tells you. That grief, when mixed with guilt, creates an echo chamber. And if you don't silence it, it becomes your new reality.

Reflection: The Guilt That Echoes

This chapter isn't about deleting apps. It's about facing the guilt that comes from seeing someone you love in pain—and believing *you* caused it.

I didn't stop checking her page because I stopped loving her.

I stopped because I couldn't carry the weight of both our grief anymore.

If you're reading this, and you're where I was—watching someone you once loved slip into sadness, depression, withdrawal—and you're convinced that it's all your fault, I want you to hear this clearly:

You are not the sole author of someone else's pain.

We all bring weight into a relationship. We all have moments we wish we could take back. But love, even imperfect love, doesn't automatically equal destruction.

Haley had her own storms. I had mine. And maybe we collided instead of healed. But I love her. Deeply. Still. And I know she loved me. The rest—the guilt, the spiral, the echo chamber—is just the grief talking.

And grief is a damn liar when it teams up with an algorithm.

So if you're refreshing her page one more time tonight, hoping for a sign that she's okay—or punishing yourself with proof that she's not—I want you to ask yourself this:

Is this helping her?

Or is it just hurting you?

Because if nothing changes, nothing changes.

And it's okay to stop bleeding for someone... even if you'd still take a bullet for them.

Chapter 12 Therapy and Putting in the Work

No one claps for the man who logs into therapy from the front seat of his truck.

There's no applause for crossing a state line into Wisconsin just to find enough signal and solitude to tell a stranger everything that's tearing you apart. No one sees the snow falling outside the windshield, or the way your hands tremble on the steering wheel—not from the cold, but from the weight of what you're about to say.

I didn't start therapy because I had some grand realization. I started because Haley asked me to. After we got back together last year, she wanted me to confront childhood trauma I hadn't dealt with. I agreed, not because I believed in it at the time, but because I believed in us. I wanted to do the work.

But week after week, instead of unpacking the past, I found myself talking about the present—about her gambling. About how nothing was changing. About how trust was slipping through my hands every time I discovered another lie.

Through ice and snow, through blistering heat and pounding rain, I'd drive a mile over the bridge and park in the same lot, week after week, pouring my heart out to someone I had never met in person. It wasn't about digging through my childhood. It was about surviving my reality.

I remember one session in particular, when the therapist asked if I'd ever drawn a red line.

A red line is different than a boundary. A boundary can bend, flex, be renegotiated. But a red line... it's the edge of the cliff. The point where something has to change—or it's over.

It felt like a sentence handed down by a judge. Not because I didn't agree—but because I knew the moment I set it, I had to be willing to follow through. No more ifs. No more maybe she'll get better. Just a cold, clear line between staying and self-preservation.

That was what therapy became for me. Not a couch and a tissue box. But a prison of decisions I didn't want to make—but had to.

Facing the Mirror

Therapy didn't offer quick relief. It didn't erase the ache in my chest or make the sleepless nights disappear. But it gave me language for the things I had been afraid to say out loud.

Like how I felt disrespected every time I found out she gambled again.
Like how hard it was to set that red line and still feel like I was betraying someone I loved.
Like how much it hurt to realize that sometimes love isn't enough to fix what someone won't face.

No one else could make me say those things. But therapy didn't let me run from them.

There is no monument to Saint Jason, and there shouldn't be. I'm not writing this book to polish my image. I'm writing it because there are men right now staring at their own dashboards, fists clenched, stomachs knotted, wondering if they're allowed to hurt this badly when they're supposed to be the strong ones.

I want them to know: it's okay to cry. It's okay to ask for help. And it's okay to choose yourself when no one else will.

What "Work" Really Looks Like

Putting in the work doesn't always look like healing trauma. Sometimes, it looks like protecting yourself from *new* trauma.

It looks like saying no to the same cycle. Like breaking the pattern. Like saying: "This is where it ends, even if I still love you."

It's sitting in a parked truck, whispering hard truths into a phone while your breath fogs up the window.

It's resisting the urge to beg someone to change when you finally realize the person who needs to change is *you*—because you're the one still bleeding out from the same wound.

It's learning that setting a red line isn't cruelty—it's the last act of self-respect when everything else has failed.

Therapy didn't fix me.
But it helped me stop breaking myself.

Reflection: What Healing Really Looked Like

It wasn't a breakthrough moment. There was no lightning bolt. No TV show version of healing where everything clicks and peace rushes in like a flood.

It was sitting in a parked truck, one mile into Wisconsin, talking to a therapist I'd never met in person. It was admitting things I didn't want to say out loud. Owning the damage I'd done. Talking through the broken record of betrayal, relapse, and hope that never lasted. It was learning what a boundary really means—and drawing that red line not to punish her, but to protect myself.

It was doing the work Haley asked me to do before she ever left. I just never expected the work to lead me here.

Healing didn't feel like strength. It felt like survival. Like saying *no more* while your heart screamed *just one more chance*. It felt like trying to be honest in a world that didn't reward it. Like grieving someone who was still alive, still posting, still breathing—just no longer yours.

And still... I kept showing up.

Because sometimes healing isn't a path forward. It's a mile marker that says: "You made it this far. Don't stop now."

I've written this mostly for men like me, because I know how easy it is to go silent, to shoulder it all, to think asking for help makes you weak. But if you're a woman reading this—or anyone who sees yourself in this pain—please know: you're seen too.

The language might be mine. But the ache? That belongs to all of us.

And if you're in that parking lot right now—somewhere between where you were and where you don't know how to go—just know this:

You're not broken beyond repair.

You're just healing in real time.

Final Note: If You're Still With Me

If you've made it this far, I want to thank you—not just for reading, but for staying.

Whether you found this book on a dashboard, in a glove box, at a rest stop, or in the darkest chapter of your own story, I hope you felt seen somewhere in these pages.

I didn't write this as a clean, polished memoir. I wrote it as a lifeline. A living journal. A flashlight passed between souls in the night.

Maybe your grief looks different than mine. Maybe it's not divorce. Maybe it's addiction, loss, shame, burnout, trauma—or something so heavy you haven't even named it yet.

But if no one else has said it lately:
You matter.
You're not too far gone.
You're not alone.

This book isn't here to save you. But it might remind you that it's okay to keep going. To keep breathing. To reach out. To rest. To fall apart and still rebuild.

You don't have to do it perfectly. You just have to do it **one mile at a time**.

And if you ever forget why that matters, just flip back to any page. I promise, there's a version of me somewhere in here who's sat exactly where you are.

Still here.
Still fighting.
Still trying.

Take care of yourself. I'll see you tomorrow. —Jason

Chapter 13: Your Miles

This book was never meant to be one-sided.
Now it's your turn.
Use the space that follows to write your own mile markers—your own truths, your own healing, your own mess, your own light.

Whatever it is, let it be real.

Because someone out there needs your story, too.

Journal Page:

Date: _____

Journal Page:

Date: _____

Journal Page:

Date: _____

Journal Page:

Date: _____

Journal Page:

Date: _____

Journal Page:

Date: _____